17/68

To Ingegerd

A little token with
love from Bill.

Christmas 1968

WHITEHORN'S
SOCIAL SURVIVAL

WHITEHORN'S
Social Survival

Katharine Whitehorn

Drawings by Mel Calman

Methuen

First published in 1968 by Methuen and Co. Ltd
© 1968 by The Observer and Katharine Whitehorn

Made and Printed in Great Britain by
Butler & Tanner Ltd, Frome and London

Acknowledgement
Most of the text by Katharine Whitehorn in this
book and most of the drawings by Mel Calman
originally appeared in The Observer Colour
Magazine.

CONTENTS

Introduction

Anyone who writes anything even remotely connected with social manners knows to wear their bullet-proof vest for the next few months; but for all that, the passions the subject arouses never cease to astonish me. Some people obviously feel affronted at the very idea of trying to manipulate social relations; they think that any such attempt must simply falsify them. Another bunch, I suspect, are reminded of their own un-ease by *any* discussion of social ease – and goodness knows I sympathise with them. And many people feel that if you talk at all about how to behave, you must in some way be urging people to ape the manners of social classes to which they don't belong – forgetting that, even if you were, it would simply enable more people to tunnel faster into more situations, and so undermine the social structure still further. Whatever the reason, it seems that while death and sex have become social small change, social small change has become taboo.

All these reactions appeared when the articles on which this book is based came out in *The Observer* – in what, to those with children and scissors, is known as the cut-out supplement. Along with the schoolgirls asking what they did with their greying underwear in the daylight of the morning after, we heard from fevered readers who imagined themselves afflicted with all the social dilemmas at once – and that was the line taken in a priceless article by Alan Brien in the *New Statesman*, himself the arch-priest of social collapse and the self-styled founder of the armpit school of criticism. Along with the headmistress who withdrew her co-operation on another article on the grounds that no respectable person would now wish to be associated with the paper (signing herself stiffly Yours in Christ) we had a sneer in a strip-cartoon from *The Listener*, and the splendid spoof from *Varsity* which appears on the inside back flap of the jacket. Hideous problems and even more hideous solutions were suggested to us, and the headache was the same as with the original: keep it clean and they say you're being unrealistic, put it all in and they say it's disgusting. It is, of course.

Those who don't like it, however, can console themselves with the absolutely disastrous effect the thing has had on my own social life. I used to pass in a crowd; now my friends wait with evil glee for me to turn up on the wrong night, address my hostess by someone else's name, eat my salad with a teaspoon and spill my drink. It's small wonder I'm now only at ease among strangers. I have never been more grateful for anonymity in my life, however, than on the day the article first appeared, and I was sitting in an aeroplane; and there was this man reading it, and I was behind him desperately trying to stop my baby rubbing his shining bald head with a rusk. For this dilemma, nobody has yet found an answer.

Katharine Whitehorn

The confidence trick

Nothing is more tiresome than the people who assume that it is useless to talk about social behaviour, because if you have confidence anything goes. Of course; but how do you get the confidence in the first place? Some just know they are superior: they are Senior Wranglers, first cousin to the Earl of Dunnocks or Born Before Their Time. Some are genuinely serene: they *are* at ease and it all comes from inside. For the rest of us, social ease comes with practice; from having lived through an increasing number of situations in which, at the time, we wished to drop dead. And I speak as one who first went into a smart hairdresser and *knelt* at the backwash.

We all go through it. But is there anything to speed up the process or make it less painful? The thing divides, as I see it, into two halves: what to do, and how to do it. It's no good knowing that a lady goes through a door first if she walks straight into a piece of plate glass; useless to know that it's considered unsmart to put your gloves in your handbag if all you do instead is drop them into the punchbowl. Time was when you were supposed to *know* what to do. The thing was linked to being born at a given social level, and to ask questions at all was a giveaway. Now things are different. Not because there are no social distinctions, but because there are far more of them, and they overlap: the moneyed overlap with the blue-blooded, the smart with both; and the essential difference is that it is now *all right to ask.*

You ask your hostess what to wear – and when she says, 'Oh, any old thing' (the rat) you pin her down to what *she* is going to wear. You ask who'll be there. You ask a trained secretary how to address a viscount on an envelope. You ask the women's magazines whether the bride's mother pays for the cake. When you go away for the weekend, you ask if it's horses, swimming or just weeding and walks. The first, last and

is it horses or swimming this weekend?

only rule on what to do in a given situation is: find out.

Doing it is different; and this hasn't changed. Swinging teenagers still come out in spots for fear the girls won't like them; applicants for new jobs continue to leave their combs in the Tube; the most confident students still go into cocktail parties where no one knows they're President of the Protest and sweat with fear as before.

Social relationships, in a word, have not suddenly become easy because people are less likely to be despised for eating with their fingers.

What, then, makes them run smoothly? Who is the happy mixer, the person who doesn't spend his time praying for invisibility or sobbing with loneliness? The answer, unfortunately, is going to sound both solemn and obvious: the people

---

Highly suspect phrases

'You will keep this to yourself, won't you?' – *Why should she? You're not.*

'I was only telling the truth!' – *You were saying the curtains were too short. You weren't saying 'I am telling you your curtains are too short because I have a hangover/no curtains myself/a dentist's appointment in half an hour.'*

'I'm so interested in people.' *Do you expect your audience to say 'Personally I prefer things?'*

---

who get on are the people who can get their mind off their own predicament and think of someone else. It is a trick, like keeping the mind on a fixed point to avoid seasickness; but it is a trick linked to psychology and apparently it works.

It has a thousand versions, but the trick is basically simple. Keep your mind on expanding the other person's ego. Pass on a pleasant remark – they glow kindly towards you; criticise, and they feel bad. Say your child is brilliant and their minds wander; imply that theirs is the clever one and they feel you're a pleasant person to have around. You start telling someone about your life and struggles. Maybe they're interested; fine. But if you ask them about theirs, why, they are delighted to discover that *they* are apparently fascinating. 'In heaven they may bore you. In hell, *you* will bore *them*.' The other person wants to feel the fascinating one. Of course this is only

11

the way to start; turn it into a way of life (as Dale Carnegie did) and you haven't much alter-

---

The dullest subjects in the world

Cars

Children

Taxes

Any sport

My pet

Why my life is so much more awful than anyone else's.

Strict ration: two sentences on each unless you are quite sure you are talking to someone similarly afflicted (and even then they won't listen, of course).

---

native but to become a total saint or a hypocrite. But in social situations it's the opening moves that matter.

This is the stupid paradox of the whole business; that we fall over ourselves trying to be cleaner, smoother, better dressed, better read, richer and more suitably brought up than the next person, and the exact opposite is what endears us to other people. Obviously you don't want to be so inefficient that it's embarrassing, or so cowed that people feel you are hardly a worthy audience. But we all want to feel great; we all love the people who make us feel great. And the only really august people we can even stand are the ones who have that rare knack of making us feel of value.

This is why the one social lapse for which there is no forgiveness is forgetting people's names –

it makes them feel that they are small and un-memorable. This is why the classic formula for a failed dinner party is three lions and no Christians to listen; why the best compliment anyone gets is 'You're someone I can *tell* things to'. This is why the way to get people to do something is to praise them for already doing it: not *'Must* you be out of the office as the clock strikes five?' but

---

You cannot go wrong

Admiring a woman's jewellery.

Asking a man about his work (unless he's unemployed or in MI5).

Sending a female flowers.

Asking a man's (non-professional) advice.

Asking for a recipe.

Saying 'I'd love to' if issued with a general invitation. It commits you to nothing.

'It's so nice to have someone around who is more interested in the job than the clock'; not 'Do we have to have this pie?' but 'Darling, you do salads so well.'

This is why Spock sells a million copies and every other child-care book makes you pray the experts' children end up bedwetting in jail: because *they* say, 'Do this. Do that', and *he* says, 'I think on the whole I probably would.' When all's said and done, it's not the Countess of Dartmouth that has the real key to the question. It's the girl in Ronald Searle's book 'The Female Approach': 'The Office of Works! Do tell me about it!'

Your social currency

It is a hard fact that the world, socially speaking, never offers something for nothing. People who can get on in it are always offering something that other people want, be it never so unlikely, devious or subtle. Indeed, one of the better games one can play while waiting in a corner for someone to speak to you is to work out exactly what the other guests were invited for. For their garrulous charm? For their name? To

Knife and fork manners never matter; thank-you manners do.

make up a spare man? (I often wonder if these available bachelors ever wonder why their invitations fall off as soon as they pair off – not because there's anything wrong with their girls.) Do they make the hostess feel she's being magnanimous? Does she owe them hospitality, and if so, why? What, in other words, have they got to offer?

Some people offer looks. This is something that can get you a long way if, like the beauty queens flatly reciting Shelley's 'Skylark' to show Talent as well, you have something else to offer with it: I can never understand why more mothers of pretty daughters don't put them into accounting, or mothers of brainy girls shove them into a brainless profession like modelling. The best thing to go with looks is vivacity, a good-time feeling; otherwise the chances are it has to be bed or serenity – and let's hope other women look on you as a good decoration.

One of the most endearing things you can offer is appreciation. I know someone who will always notice if you're wearing a new ring, another who will always remember to pass on a compliment; they are people who manage a better sort of sympathy because they are capable of saying 'Hooray' as well as 'Alas'. I'd like to think it goes deeper than a trick, but it certainly works. Beware, though, of contrasting the other person's excellence with your own inferiority too much; it never rings true for long.

You can be an entertainment. You can be a cabaret, a one-man band, a flood of marvellous, ebullient, witty talk. The Brendan Behans of this world seem able to commit just about every

other error and their friends still cope with them, drink with them, bail them out: to live under that sparkling fountain is worth any amount of inconvenience. Maybe this is beyond the rest of us. But developing a line of patter can be a great help towards crossing the barrier that separates us all from other people.

You can be helpful. There are always people who stay with us, who never get left out, because they are the marvellous, sustaining souls who get the shopping when the rest of us are ill, who can fill in the five o'clock gap in a dinner party, who will drive the old dear home. And if this is all you've got to offer, you'd better offer that. A famous authoress talks of a friend called Finkelbaum; he is so immensely helpful that he is always among those present. He is three feet

high and four feet round and he pours, she tells us, a whole bottle of eau de cologne into his bath every morning. Yet when he gets out he is still three feet high, he is still called Finkelbaum and he is still four feet round. No wonder his helpfulness is of a superior quality – it has to be.

There's a caution to this one, of course: you don't want to overwhelm someone with favours or they'll resent it; an impression of being merely willing to help may be a better start. And someone, probably Benjamin Franklin, said you should start by getting someone to do *you* a slight favour; they so enjoy the warm, benign feeling associated with it that they are well disposed to like you.

You can offer hospitality – a bed to visiting godchildren or foreigners, a dinner to people you have met and like; few can resist a chance to eat a free meal and meet someone new – at least the first time. If you don't know enough of the people you want to know, you can be more brazen with mere acquaintances if you are giving a binge *for* something – the Spastics fund or the launching of a new book, some emigrating friends or arriving Americans, to swap children's clothes or decorate a friend's flat.

People living on their own, especially, need to learn the art of entertaining; I remember reading in an article for single women – 'Make your in-

it's not fair!
I asked them to mine only
because I wanted
to go to theirs –
and now they've
not asked me...

vitations worth accepting,' and I can think of three single women whose dinner parties are the sort for which you angle for an invitation. I must admit that they are personally charming too – but I'd go to their dinners with my tongue hanging out anyway.

The one thing it never pays to offer is gloom. 'Laugh and the world laughs with you,' and all that; you listen to a friend's miseries maybe half a dozen times; after that she had better occasionally touch on some other subject or her presence becomes a chore. 'Oh, I sing for my supper, all right,' said the bachelor of a certain age, pouring someone else's claret – but we all sing for our supper. It's just a question of what song you sing – and of knowing songs that can be learnt.

How to improve your currency

Try the gimmick gimmick

You are the person who always has a vast old Victrola or a tame mystic; you have a red beard; you are the man who vowed never to wash till we had a Liberal Prime Minister; you can recite the whole of 'Omar Khayyam' or the works of Edward Ruark (only don't, for heaven's sake, actually do so). Gets you tabbed in people's memory; gives people something to say about you. Worth it, even if you drop the thing like a discarded snake skin as soon as you've out-grown it (if you ever do).

You are a public convenience

I don't quite mean in the sense in which some-one I heard of once found two sodden characters pathetically ringing his doorbell with the words: 'We're friends of Martin's, where can we be sick?' But if you are the only person they know with reference books, or have the only transport, and must be included; if you are the only person on the stair who never runs out of Alka-Seltzer or cigarettes, or has stamps, a telephone, a Good Address, then you have a credit balance: you have someone to talk to anyway.

18

You are part of the calendar

If you can by hook or by crook be the person
with the tickets for Twickenham or Glynde-
bourne, the girl whose aunt gets you into the
Royal Enclosure, the person whose vast drunken
birthday picnic becomes something people don't
like to be left out of, you're away. If you
are utterly unmemorable yourself, get the
whole bedsit block to celebrate something
like Beethoven's Birthday or Sadie Hawkins
Day.

You are available

Shy young men who have the sense to skip the
dishy dollies for the time being (they won't look
at them just yet, anyway) and concentrate on
flattering married women of a certain age get
asked to an awful lot of dinners; and many a
man has been spare escort to a flatful of girls,
treated like an amiable St Bernard by everyone,
and suddenly scooped in the fascinating new
girl with one snap of his over-prepared jaws.
Same the other way round: washing the shirts
of a couple of dopes at least gets you into a place
where men are to be found.

But join the right club – that is, the wrong one. I can't think why more men don't go to cookery classes or girls have the sense to join clubs for things like Law Reform or Model Making, which mainly attract men.

Avoiding devaluation

Even for those who *have* got all the introductions, there are attitudes and attributes which can make you persona non-starter from the social point of view. Into this category come the wets – they complain that the world doesn't come to them; they sit in their rooms wondering why no one asks them out of them; when they arrive they sit there waiting to be amused – and I daresay we've all been wets in our time. There are the snakes, who are charming when they're there but totally unreliable: everything makes tattle somewhere else. Snakes have to be very, very amusing to be asked again. And there are the social bulldozers, who never stop talking, who are going to do their Liberace imitation come what may, who insist on sailing into the back kitchen to fetch the ice from behind the chaos you'd rather they didn't see.

Two other categories that make hostesses wince are those who habitually indecently expose their opinions, and those who lash out in defence of them. As one who does, unforgivably, lose her temper in public I know what I'm talking about here; and the sad fact of the matter is that rage on an abstract matter is practically never justified – and never wise, if you want to be asked again. The only exception is an attack on a friend: if you say 'He's a friend of mine, please don't go on' and the person does, the bad manners are then his no matter what you

throw at him. (A good host ought to be able to prevent it, actually, by changing the subject very firmly indeed; but most of them, either from devilry or paralysis, tend to sit there and let it happen.) And you have to be very charming indeed in other ways if it is known that everyone present must devote their whole energy to keeping you off your pet subject, be it biological warfare, mental health, the need for nursery schools or the Society for the abolition of Norman St John Stevas. The fact that you may be Right is not the point.

Are you on your own?

A good part of all this chat has been about what you should do to please/amuse/placate/consolidate your friends; but what if you haven't got any? Nobody ever admits to this, but I know the symptoms. The girl who hurries urgently from the office in the evening, looking neither to right nor left, is the one with nowhere to go; the man whose crammed diary is full of

Perhaps I have got mental B.O?

entries like 'Cleaner calls' or '10.15 see Jenkins in office' is the lonely one; the girl who seems forever banging about the communal sink but bolts when you speak to her is the one who is so corroded with loneliness she's forgotten how to talk. What do *they* do?

The first thing is to stop being choosy. Phrases like 'I'm not the club-going type' or 'I don't want to have coffee with just other housewives' or 'They're all terribly old and square' conceal too high expectations; you came to town expecting to chat with Cilla Black or parry Kenneth Allsop with a couple of choice sentences, and there seems no point in talking to the old girl up from Swansea at the next table in the Lyons.

But there is. For one thing, you can get so out of practice. After a year in Finland where I couldn't speak their language I became practically incapable of speaking my own; you have to keep the habit of chatter going. Avoid supermarkets; go to the library at a time when the girl at the desk has time to talk; buy your evening paper from people who think they are 'characters' and gas accordingly.

For another, you have to start somewhere. I'm not saying the old lady will rise up, throw off her rags like a crone in a fairy tale and say, 'I'm Edith Evans in disguise – come and have dizzy drinks in Albany.' But the blighted office junior has a brother who is a wood-worker who knows a man who grows trees who *is* someone you find likable; the next man in the pub has a wife and you give her a hand heaving him into bed and she asks you to a party . . . Remember the great Jack Gallagher dictum: 'We all of us have terrible friends; we are all of us somebody's terrible friends.' Almost nobody's social circle is an unbroken O of Giotto; and think what common cause you will have with any other odd man out – though it is still not considered a good social opening to start 'I think our hostess is a louse.'

There is also the cruel fact that you get what you put in, and if you scorn anyone below what you think is your own social rating you'll be in trouble if it ever goes down. One of the most sought-after women I know, well over 70, has always been the one to have the crippled cousin to stay or be there when Mother has mumps (those who are there when Father has mumps are just a bunch of evil old ravens). Stick to your own kind, and it will all be very brilliant – or very suicidal. But if you reckon that anyone has some sort of claim to kindness, you may yourself end up at the receiving end of a very sensible idea.

The social scene

Invitations

The only thing that really matters about invitations is that they should make it clear whether you are going to get fed or not. An invitation for 8 o'clock may be after-dinner drinks or a supper party; don't leave it to guesswork. Put 'supper and drinks' or 'wine and cheese' or 'coffee and beer'. Same for informal spoken ones: make it obviously *after* or *before*: an aunt of mine had a couple turn up for drinks at 7; she meant pre-dinner drinks, they meant after-tea and stayed all evening. If you've had too few answers by a couple of days before, ring up.

Arriving late

There are three stages of lateness: 1. Only just, in which case excuses are pointless. 2. Pretty late: if you are habitually late, it doesn't matter what excuse you give, they won't believe you – sure the car broke down, but doesn't it always?

3. So late they'd almost given you up and are vastly relieved to see you. You'd better offer an excuse, but briefly – they don't want to listen to a great saga as well. And don't forget that for most cook-hostesses utter punctuality is even more disastrous than lateness.

Introductions

Every book gives painstaking rules for this; as nobody ever remembers them they can't matter very much. For what it's worth, you start with the name of the most important female: 'Lady Bracknell, this is . . .'

If you've forgotten names

Introduce the other person – 'You know my husband, don't you?' Some try subtleties like saying, 'I've forgotten both your names' and then explaining afterwards to each that it was the other's they'd forgotten; I think this makes too heavy weather of the whole thing. Alternatively, you can say 'Introduce yourselves, I can smell something burning' and dash.

What is often overlooked is that these situations can frequently be seen coming and headed off. You are talking to the man and know you can't remember who he is – try phrases like 'What are you working on now?' or 'Where *was* it we met last?' so that their answer gives you a clue – 'Heart Transplants', or 'the Rhodesia account' or 'the diurnal response in aphitoid butterflies' on the one hand, or 'the Queen Mary', 'Buckingham Palace' or 'that dreadful party of Sybil's' on the other.

If, too, you know a little ahead the problem that's going to hit you, you can sometimes be making a remark at the moment of impact which

enables you to say 'Hrrmph works with beetles' or 'she's in the Foreign Office, I should explain' which gives the person at least a gratifying sense that you know perfectly well who they are, even if you have forgotten their n. or m.

When people ring up to apologise

Much the nicest thing is to answer in bewilderment: 'What on earth for? Oh, that? I'd forgotten all about it.'

What to wear

Ask. Hostess can wear dottier clothes than guests. Hell, she needs some compensations. Remember that, other things being equal, clothes are more formal in the provinces than in London.

Dinner

There's a remarkable similarity between dinner-parties at very different levels. The only tricky problem seems to be whether, at the end of the meal, you sit tight, all move together or separate men from women. In older households, women can sit over the coffee in the drawing-room for 20 minutes or more; the great thing is not to let all the women sit in a bunch or they'll have to *stay* talking to women all evening. Sitting at table may be uncomfortable (depends on the chairs) and leaves you stuck with the one person unless your host rather artificially moves

---

Five Golden Rules

1 Never ask for anything you can't see – in the food and drink line, I mean; I'm not talking about gentlemen who prefer blondes.

2 If you've made one good joke, stop there (and don't repeat the punch-line).

3 Do not have an all-male or all-female conversation – hair, the war, guns, fabric, etc. – in mixed company.

4 Never agree with anyone who is insulting their own nearest and dearest; both will turn and rend you.

5 When in doubt, shut up and smile.

---

you about. Best way out is an adaptation of the old custom: women move off first, but only to have first crack at the bathroom and ask as they sit on their hostess's bed, 'My dear, who *is* that fascinating man?' Coffee for all together after about 15 minutes.

When to go

Stick it out for three hours from the invitation time unless plainly very ill or very old. Longer if you like, of course.

How to get them to go

Empty all the ashtrays in a pointed manner; stay standing.

One host I heard of appears to fall asleep; he then wakes with a jerk and says, 'Darling, I think we should be going now.' Alas, I suppose you couldn't work it too often.

Thank you

I note with gloom that more and more people tend to write thank-you notes for dinners. Compromise, with old friends, is to ring up and rehash the evening with joy. You must say thank you if you dropped a brick (but don't mention it), if you know the people only slightly, if they are evidently blue-blooded and likely to expect it, or if they thanked *you* last time.

Lunch parties

(and don't you tell me I ought to say luncheon).

Only problem: when to leave. About two hours from time of invitation unless you're sharing a sloppy Sunday with friends, in which case you may well be invited to tea.

Teenagers' parties

Will be run by teenagers, who will tell you what to do. Resist attempts to get you out of the house completely if there has been any instance of wholesale gate-crashing in the neighbourhood: no one can get these hordes out, but a firm father can and should stop them getting in.

Children's parties

A world of its own. Get Rosemary Say's pamphlet 'Preparing a Children's Party' (Encyclopedia Britannica, 4s 6d).

Cocktail parties

If you must. Don't do it on wine alone if you can help it; it's slow to warm up: 'Candy is dandy but liquor is quicker' – and he didn't say Chilean Moselle. Give the drunks among your friends

progressively weaker drinks. There will always be a hard core left over at nine, to be fed either out or in; don't try to disinclude people at this stage, it can't be done tactfully.

Party problems

What do you do ...

When your wife hisses 'Drinks' and the first guest says 'Whisky, please, I MUST tell you about the other day when I saw old Frog-morton . . .' Your first duty is to the thirsts of the others. Say firmly 'This I want to hear' but dash off.

What do you do . . .

When you are at a party and someone intro-duces you to your worst enemy? You make the best of it; exchange civilised dialogue. You do not turn on your heel with a sharp hiss; it's too hard on whoever introduced you.

What to do if you know nobody

Hang about on the fringes of the most open-spaced group and laugh at the jokes. If a single figure detaches itself, say 'Are you a great friend of – name the host?' This requires an answer at least; you take it from there. Phrase for accost-ing total strangers: 'Do you know a lot of people here?'

What do you do ...

When your husband is telling a long, boring anecdote? Look fascinated. The others may then think (a) that the story may have a redeeming punch line or (b) that you haven't heard it before.

What do you do ...

When you are being bored at a party? Don't show it. They don't know that what you are listening to isn't much fun *except* by your expression. And if you seem to be having a good time, you are more likely to catch the eye of someone more amusing. Rescue operations are a good deal more rare than they should be.

What do you do ...

If you are standing there doing no harm to anybody rather congratulating yourself on coping with drink, bag, gloves and cigarette, and someone hands you a plate of food? And a napkin? And a fork? You use the left hand as a four-tiered rack. Handbag handles over the wrist; gloves over little finger; then napkin; then cigarette; then plate with canapé upon it; and also glass, held firmly down by the thumb; keeping right hand free for shaking. Of course you should get rid of the cigarette first, but it's not always possible. Actually you can skip gloves nowadays and people don't often notice except in snowstorms.

Drink

If it's you, you probably don't notice it. If it's your spouse, remove him/her without remarking on it – it's perfectly possible other people, less practised in detecting the signs, or well away themselves, hadn't even noticed.

Staying away

Get as much information as possible about what's going to happen. Guests who spend part of their time amusing themselves are the most welcome; but it's a good idea to say, 'I thought I'd go and lie down for a couple of hours', so that your hostess can then say 'Fine. We're leaving for Sandy's at about 3.30' rather than have her beat up and down the hall frantically waiting for you to appear. Good guests make their own bed, offer help in the house and STOP offering it if it's turned down. They bring something useful to eat – pâté or a box of chocolates; if they're going to bring a game pie, they warn beforehand, or how is their hostess to fit it in? for elevenses?

Going to bed

There is, I'm told, a convention that it's up to the guest to go to bed first. But nobody knows about it, so it isn't much use. The only sensible thing is for anyone who feels like it to yawn and say 'Well, I think I'll turn in, if you don't mind.' It's ten to one the other party, unaware of the

rules, was waiting for this to be said. Or a hostess can start saying things like 'Do you like a hot-water bottle?' and 'What do you like for breakfast?'

Tipping

You used to leave something on the dressing-table for the servants, and you still do it if there are any. But nowadays it's usually safest to ask

your hostess whether, and how much, because who knows whether that Italian help was au pair, servant, girl from the village or future daughter-in-law. Always go slightly above what she tells you.

Thank you

Bread-and-butter letter a must – phone call won't do.

Work

People usually feel more at ease at work than anywhere else: the two bad moments are simply the interview and the first few days. It's mean, by the way, to run down the outfit someone else works for. Either he agrees with you, in which case you're simply sneering at him for being unable to get a better job; or he doesn't, in which case you make him cross.

Interview

The snag here is that the first basic principle of good behaviour – hand the other man the ball – can't work here; he's trying to get something out of *you*. One-word answers make you dull; you can't very well ask him about his roses or his old school tie. You can ask with fascination about the job – not the teabreaks but the responsibility, not the money but (O marvellously nebulous word) the scope. By the time he's finished telling you the whole truth about glazing eggcups or whatever it is, he may think it's you who know.

Girls and the boss

This is always cracked up to be a much worse problem than it is. Only in occasionally letting you go out of the lift first does he concede that you get treated as a female. Otherwise you are an employee, and nothing else, unless the situation is developing in other ways.

What to do when the boss is talking nonsense

Remember the shining example of the man in Evelyn Waugh's 'Scoop' who used to say 'Very true, Lord Copper', when the boss was right and 'Up to a point, Lord Copper', when the boss was wrong. No one likes being contradicted, so it's better to sound defeated and semi-convinced: 'Yes. Yes, I suppose that's right. It's just that I'd been wondering whether . . .'

Dress

Exactly the way all his other employees dress but with one difference – an interesting tie, a weird handbag. Don't loll back in the chair; don't sit edgily on the front of it; and try to conceal your absolutely maddening habit of brushing your hair out of your eyes every 10 seconds until he's actually signed on the dotted line. And smile.

First job

You can't make a good impression on the first day, but you can make a bad one; the only real rule is go slow. Be overwhelmed. Be shy. (If in an executive position, be inscrutable.) Smile on the second day, and ask advice on the third. And

do find out what the job is before wading in to do it all – *The Observer* still remembers someone several years ago who threw away all the features editor's files in the first week in an excess of zeal.

The telephone

Considering how long the thing's been in use, it's extraordinary how badly people still use it. Once you get to his secretary, say who you are before you ask if you can speak to the boss. If you don't know him well, tell the secretary what it's all about, briefly; ask him to call back at a convenient moment to talk. What on earth's the sense in bulldozing through if he's in a meeting or the lavatory? Any secretary worth her salt can keep hated callers at bay for days at a time.

Do *not* say 'Er – you won't remember me, I think, but we did meet once at Jean's; well, anyway, I thought I'd better ring you . . . it's about these welfare homes – oh dear I can't think *straight* this morning, the girl's got mumps . . . well anyway . . .' Say: 'My name is Elsie

Smithers; I wanted to have a word with you about homes for spastics. Is this a good moment or shall I call back?' And when you've finished, recap the only important point and *ring off*, 'See you on the first, then' or 'Thanks so much, that's been a great help'. Every time I get a crossed line I wait with baited breath to see how they'll finish – often you hear them inviting each other to a lunch they don't want and will probably later cancel simply because they can't think of any other way to end the conversation.

How to talk

More than half of all social ease depends on opening the mouth and pushing something out of it. But *what*? Nothing is more paralysing than the sort of conversation that goes:

Have you seen 'The Boy Friend'?
No.
Have you seen 'Carmen'?

37

No – I like the cinema more actually.
Oh – have you seen 'Loin de Vietnam'?
No.

Or the same thing played out in huntin',

shootin', golfin' terms. Attempts to launch
directly into subjects can lead to these ghastly
impasses.

So? So talk round them. As thus: 'Have you
seen "The Boy Friend"? ' 'No, I kept missing it.
They say the hems don't look nearly as short
now as they did when it first came out.' Or 'Do
you hunt?' 'No, I've never been able to look a
horse in the eye. Do tell me – did you always
love riding or did you only begin to love it when
you were grown up?'

If they keep talking about books you haven't
read, ask do they feel differently about books in
limited editions or paperbacks? Do they mind
whether they *possess* books? Ask if they ever get
the giggles in libraries? If they go on about
records, ask them how do they imagine themselves when they hear them – dancing, loving,
conducting? Get *off* the part of the subject about
which you can't say anything – there's always a
way out somewhere.

So, supposing for once you are well away, and they start glazing over – worse, do they always start glazing over? Plenty of people suffer from total recall when they're at their shyest – remember to put the brakes on, and let them make the running if they're actually interested. A golden rule, unless you are already Lord Boothby or Dee Wells or Malcolm Muggeridge or somebody, is: 'Leave your monologue till later.' Much later. Like the oration at your own funeral.

What do you say...

To strangers

Go warily. You know nothing about them – it is easier now than at any other time to put your foot in it. Ask them about themselves by all means – and don't denounce Roman Catholics, psychologists, Jews or Enoch Powell before you've made quite sure you're not talking to one. Remember that *all* jokes about people called Pigg, Crichton, Edward Behr, Strongarm, Ethelred the Unready or the *other* Marlon Brando have already been made.

In trains? 'When in Rome, do as the Romans

do; and when I am in Britain I always try to give the impression that I have died in my seat.' Actually some people like to be talked to. Try a smile and single remark about the weather or the lateness of the train. If they follow it up, go ahead. Remember: as with animals, they're probably as scared of you as you are of them. FOOTNOTE: If your stranger seems eminent, always say 'Not *the* John Smith?' It's easy enough for him to say 'No, one of the others.' And you're covered.

When your hairpiece comes off in his hand

There's only one thing you can say: 'Now *all* my defences are down.' It's up to you whether or not you laugh as you say it.

To the bereaved

Don't gasp nervously if the subject of the lost one comes up. Far more people than you think genuinely want to talk about it, indeed must talk about it, and hate bottling it up. But if they switch off quickly, take their hint. If they weep, offer a handkerchief in silence; you could say you're glad they feel they can cry in front of you.

To the separated

Do *not* take the occasion to ask unforgivable questions about their sex life or say how much you loathed the fellow anyway. For one thing, they may always come together again; for another, plenty of separations arranged with a fair degree of amity have been made lacerating mainly by 'kind' friends leaping in with both feet.

To the divorced

Offer to hold their hand through the court proceedings and your reward is sure in heaven. Start treating them as attractive single people for social purposes; don't just ask them round to tea with the children. And don't ask them to parties with their ex. They may not mind, but they are *bound* to have a better time without.

To the deaf

Speak clearly – usually more important than speaking very loud. And remember, most do some lip-reading, even unconsciously; get the

It's so peaceful to turn off when you like...

light on your face, turn towards them and take the fag out of your mouth. *Do not* behave as if their understanding were affected.

To the blind

The two things the blind hate most are people addressing their mothers, wives, etc., with 'Would he like to . . .?' when they are standing there; and being helped across the road in a vice-like grip as if they were little children liable to break away. Have some sense.

To children

I'm inclined to think that social ease with children is something you can't fake and there's no point in trying. But you can avoid a few obvious pitfalls – so obvious that you can't think why people constantly crash into them. Don't, for example, rush up and hug a child who is not

a dear friend – they have their dignity. Don't talk about them as if they weren't there. Don't praise the baby and leave out the elder – and that goes for presents, too. And if you are utterly at sea with them, talk to them as if they are grown-ups. It's probably nearer the mark than your idea of what's suitable for children.

To people older or younger

Special problems crop up when you are talking to someone much older or much younger, but actually – except that you have to SPEAK UP when talking to the aged – the rules are the same both ways round. Just as you mustn't talk about money to people richer or poorer, you mustn't talk about dates to people older or younger. Nothing is more tedious to the young than your memories of Marie Lloyd in her younger days (if the youngster *is* a theatre historian he will no doubt say so), similarly no one but an ape talks about the Monkees to anyone over 40 (35? 25? 14?). Just keep clear of the subjects which draw the age barrier, and talk about something of

general interest. For what it's worth, though, it can be stated that the young most frequently irritate the old by proposing devastating new solutions to the world's problems which were also proposed – and demolished – in the fifth century B.C.; and that the old most irritate the young by their apparent disapproval of everything whatsoever that's been thought up since the war. A little disguise might help.

Awkward questions

What are you doing on Thursday?

– and you don't know if it's babysitting or the theatre. Only way out: firm commitment of a vague nature – 'I'm meeting my aunt', 'I have to collect a suitcase', 'We're going over to Highgate'. Then when you hear what's proposed, you can always say, 'Well, we ought to be back by then.'

How do you like my new picture?

'It's very striking'; 'Goes beautifully with the room'. 'Strange' – on a long-drawn-out note – 'I wish I knew as much about art as you do.'

What do you think of our country?

This is always dreadful because the person asking it is generally so touchy. All honour to Paul Usher, who found the perfect answer although confronted by three Egyptians of different political beliefs and an Englishman who still thought General Gordon was around. He said, 'I admire the spirit of your young people.'

The sex circus

This is the hardest area to give suggestions for, partly because the mores of different groups vary so widely – tell a teenager what the divorcees do and they'd shriek with laughter,

44

and vice-versa. And also because no one really knows what other people do – they know what they say they do, or what Nell Dunn says they do, or what everyone *thinks* the others do. There are still, perhaps, a few pointers.

Next morning

Men want you clean, shining and preferably accompanied by coffee. Women desperately want reassurance. As one put it, 'A bunch of flowers next morning is worth an emerald bracelet a

week later – and who the hell ever gets a bracelet anyway?'

It's just the sign that you want: that he's remembered what happened, and is pleased. In the words of Lord Peter Wimsey, 'It is the first duty of a gentleman to remember in the morning who he went to bed with the night before.'

Propositions

In this day and age you simply cannot get away with drawing yourself up to your full width and saying 'How could you think that I was that sort of girl?' Hell, you don't want to be thought the *other* sort of girl.

But that makes it harder, if anything, to say no without making the man feel small (if you are saying no, that is). He's a human being too; there's no sense in being unduly bruising. And you don't want him to go round slanging you because you've hurt his feelings – you know the definition of a lesbian film star: one who wouldn't sleep with the photographer. There are really only two categories: either it has to be 'It's not that I don't want you but . . .' or 'I respect you but . . .' Things like 'Steady, not so fast' or 'I'd want to know you so much better . . .' 'I'm sorry, I'm just not ready for it' or 'I just don't feel we have that sort of relationship' can be brought into ploy – they don't have to be believed. It's worth remembering that, whereas a lot of men used to ask for conversation when they really wanted sex, nowadays they often feel obliged to ask for sex even when they really want conversation.

Holding the pass or what every good rancher should know

What do you do when you're having a cheery conversational evening with a girl and she suddenly stops talking and you realise you're expected to make a pass at her? And what happens when you kiss a girl you've been talking to for hours and she leaps back in startled distaste? Both crises can be handled in such a way as to restore egos all round. In the first case, *seem* to be being led away by the charm in her eyes; break off in the middle of a sentence, say 'What was I saying?' and look distracted. Then say, as if being exceedingly firm with yourself, 'No. I'm *not* going to spoil this marvellous conversation

46

just because you're so desirable. There's so few girls you can *talk* to, I mean really talk. Now about the nationalisation of iron and steel. . . .' That should appease her feelings for that evening; next time you'll at least know where you stand.

In the second, your only hope is to suggest that you are mildly *pleased* that she leapt away; that so many girls expect to be kissed, just because

---

Five things no one must ever say before, during or after

You are bad in bed

You will never be a success at your job

You're getting old

I'd rather watch television

You remind me of my mother

---

you adore talking to them; that of course it's on the intellectual plane that you prefer to operate. . . . Saves your vanity, too, by implying that you only did it to be polite.

Saying goodbye

There is one way to leave a woman that is less bruising to her than most of the others. It has often been tried successfully by the kind and the smooth, though it doesn't, of course, help any-one to leave someone they've actually married. You let the situation go downhill as far as it can – rows, missed phone calls, lateness, churlish-ness, the lot. Then, when it's got so bad she'd almost rather be without you, you suddenly break it off, at the same time giving her back your old image of her. 'We can't go on like this, it used to be so wonderful.'

You recall what it was you used to like about her (if you think you won't remember, write it down at the beginning of the affair), you give some paltry but personal present like a favourite knife of yours or a bit of rock from Stromboli. You say you'll always remember, etc. And you then push off and block, absolutely, all attempts to get through to you again. Then she may manage to feel drained but restored, instead of bruised and slighted. Worth trying anyway.

What to do when a friend's husband makes a pass at you

Ascertain whether he is drunk or sober. Decide whether it is welcome or unwelcome. Take

action according to your morals (if any) and preferences, and SHUT UP ABOUT IT.

*What to do when a friend's husband
makes a pass at someone else*

You haven't seen it. In *no circumstances* tell
her about it.

*What to do when your own husband
makes a pass at someone else*

Whatever you do about it once you get home,
the only graceful way to act at the time is to
behave as if you were the guardian of that dotty
millionaire who kept writing people cheques for
a million dollars. Tolerance not wholly un-
tinged by amusement is the note: avoid high
drama at all costs, or you might actually have
high drama on your hands.

Money

Much the most sensitive area nowadays – but
with certain accepted conventions. The great
rule is not to talk about money with people who
have much more or much less than you. Even
by implication. It makes you squirm when people
go on about their new car to those whose antique
Minis are a living tribute to the sticking power
of Sellotape; it also makes you squirm, though
not so much of course, to hear people carefully
recommending bargains which are still way out-
side someone else's scope: 'And do you know, it
was only seven guineas.' There are more ways
than one of going slumming in ermine and pearls.

If you are very rich, let the poorer party pay
occasionally – they aren't your dependants.
BUT do not casually land them with the bill for
a dinner you were supposed to be paying for

because you've come out without your cheque book. And if you *are* buying them a meal, make it clear from the start. It is agony to eat your way through wondering if you will be able to pay at the end.

If you are hard up, be careful not to miss your round too often and get a reputation for being mean, BUT don't think you have to give your classy friends grouse and pâté de foie gras if you ask them in for a snack. They may be rich but they aren't senseless, and they'll be ill at ease because they are bleeding for you.

Rich or poor, the one socially safe thing to say is how wonderful is Marks and Spencer.

Borrowing money

Everyone in the world has had to do it at one time or another. Say why you want it and when they'll get it back; and if you can't pay on the nail say why. Don't just dodge about hoping they'll have forgotten: they won't have. And for large sums, do what a friend of mine did, who insisted on giving a receipt. 'The way I drive,' he told a friend he was borrowing money from, 'I'd rather you had a legal claim against my estate.'

Class

It is popular to pretend that there aren't any class distinctions any more, if only because in the communications world the class barriers tend to operate the other way round – Etonians yelping to get in, board-school boys turning them down. And the communications people form our ideas. But it ain't necessarily so.

If you want to get it right on the more old-fashioned beat, you can get Nancy Mitford's 'Noblesse Oblige' out of the library and bone up on all the U and non-U business. If you want to avoid straightforward social solecisms, get Martine Legge's book on 'Etiquette' (Nutshell, 5s). If you want to know what Belgravia is up to (or was, at least, a few years back), 'Lady Behave', by Anne Edwards and Drusilla Beyfus, is still far the best, since it talks about an entirely post-war world and has no hangovers from the days when you could always tell a lady by her shoes and her gloves.

But you can get a bit of sense into the situation by asking yourself coldly: 'Suppose I never say "Pardon?" or "serviette" again, suppose I stop asking for the toilet even if I'm dancing up and down, and doggedly call it a pudding even if it's lemon sorbet, will Lady Snooks be fooled by my disguise? Will she assume that my father was the tenth Earl of Penthouse?' Like hell she will. So maybe it isn't worth the bother.

Dropped bricks

Don't try to pick them up again – at least not directly. There is an inexorable law which causes one to talk about imbeciles to those who have retarded children, poverty to those on the bread-line, and dowdiness to those draped in the fashions of 1950. There is only one way you can sail on to clearer waters: *keep your eyes steady*. Do *not* shy nervously; do *not* look down at the uneven hemline, do not let your glance wander to the tell-tale bandage. Then you have a chance of changing the purport of what you are saying without apparently having noticed you've said it.

Disgusting personal problems

We all have them, they cause more social misery than almost anything else, and they are unmentionable. The squeamish can stop here.

Rude noises

(and, worse still, rude smells).

If there is nothing you can do by constriction of throat or rectum to head them off, try to move away from the group you are with ('I must just find an ashtray' or 'I *say* look at that squirrel!') and create diversionary noises – snap a handbag, scrape a foot. Tummy rumbles are for some reason more OK – laugh if you can.

Wetting the pants

(which adults can often do with a really violent cough).

Cross legs hard as you breathe in for cough.

Damp palms

Simply don't shake hands – so many people never do anyway. If you're obsessed by the problem, wear a fingerstall and say you *can't*. Or develop a firmer-than-ordinary grip – it's the limp wet fish in the other person's hand that displeases.

BO

Not true that your best friend won't tell you – my smelliest friend said despairingly 'My best friends tell me *all the time*.' You have to change shirts and socks oftener; but even more import-

ant is to try to arrive early and avoid getting flustered. It's when you heat up that the trouble usually starts. Why is it, by the way, that the most BO people always stand closer than anyone else? If you pong, keep your distance.

Collapse of clothes

If your *slip* goes, and you can make it to the loo, put your bra on top of it – that should hold it. If it's your *skirt* or *trouser* hook, thread the hanging-up loop round and round the hook. If it's your *bra strap*, be brutal: make a hole in the fabric and tie the strap through. Better too up than too down. For most of us, anyway: I was once tossed in the air three times in Finnish ceremony by the members of an Anglo-Finnish club; it did for my bra strap minutes before the final group photograph. No wonder I clutched my bouquet dramatically to my heart.

Collapse of other people's clothes

Do you tell a man his flies are undone? A man can easily tell another man – so if possible whisper to another man and let him cope. If no

other man available, try 'I say, are your trousers . . .?' and then break off in the confusion you genuinely feel. It's kinder than letting him go on all evening that way. Same, the other way round, with shoulder-straps: tuck them in lovingly be they never so twisted and grey.

Pants

Usually you feel them going; grip your arms to your sides and make for the Ladies. If they actually descend, it depends where you are. At a big binge kick them off and walk away; if there's furniture, foot them under it (but remove later to avoid divorce action between your host and hostess); if concealment is hopeless, look down and say 'You can't rely on anything these days' and calmly pick them up.

Noses, teeth and nails

People are disgusted if you clear these out where they can see it; but letting them stay dirty is worse. Nails can usually be dealt with under the tablecloth or in the handbag while gaily talking on (try a much-folded bus-ticket); teeth must only be picked among blood relations or in France; the one thing you mustn't do where anybody, even your spouse, can see, is pick your nose. Saying, 'I was only scratching' is no way out. If you have to blow your nose at table, you may as well apologise. But pick your moment: remember the girl who tucked two handkerchiefs into her decolletage, soaked one, and found a sudden silence as she groped in her bosom for the second. 'I know I had two when I came,' she said helplessly.

You are going to be sick

You have a touch of Tunis tummy – make for the lavatory. Do *not* explain to one and all what is wrong; apologise quietly to your hostess later, explaining why. Always worth doing; in this day and age they may otherwise think you were the worse for drink. Worth doing even if you were, of course.

When it's chronic

Anybody can risk being disgusting by horrific accident but some people are generally disgusting – usually in entirely preventable ways. So ask yourself the following. If the answer to every question is yes, you'd better join the French Foreign Legion, or the Government or something.

Do you talk with your mouth full, eat with it open?

An awful lot of people do. If people look elsewhere when you eat, it's either this or the size of the mouthfuls.

Are you covered in warts and potholes?

Many charming people are – the less charming had better not risk it. Save up and apply to Katherine Corbett of South Molton Street, London, to take away yours as she took away (some of) mine.

Do you have a hideous habit?

What revolts one may leave another cold; but for the record, people can be completely put off if you crack a book open as if breaking its spine, put used matches back in the box (or empty milk bottles back in the fridge), pick your nose (with or without rolling the results between your finger-tips), search for old forgotten far-off things in the back of your mouth, or diligently scratch your ears with your little finger.

Some people have an uncanny knack (I'm appalled to say it runs in my family) of discussing at the table the way they were sick yesterday, what the accident looked like, how they found the child's nappy and so on. First of all ask yourself if you have to say all this *at all*; and if you do, put it off till after the meal for heaven's sake.

A few special questions

Who do I tip at a hairdresser's?

The stylist, unless it's the boss; and a smaller tip for the girl who washes your hair. You may be embarrassed but the person expecting it is not. Do not try to slide halfcrowns unobtrusively into the pockets of young male hairdressers in skin-tight trousers.

How on earth do you address irregular couples on the outsides of envelopes?

Depends on the irregular couple, of course. If they simply are not married, and you don't know what they've told their landlady, stick to Mr and Mrs. For some reason a common compromise is 'John and Mary Smith' – avoids the dread word 'Mrs'. If they are pairs of queers put both names in alphabetical order. If you simply mean that one's a peeress of the realm and the other isn't, you can, of course, look *that* up in an etiquette book: but it's simpler just to put 'David and Margaret Boodle' without title –

(only don't do what I did and put David and Bea when the chap's name was actually Sydney).

What do I do about Sunday lunch – if I invite people I never know if they're going to turn up in their gardening jeans or their Sunday best. What do I wear?

Your gardening jeans. Then if they turn up in skirts and a tie – the couple, I mean – you can

pretend you haven't got around to changing yet and flash off and do so.

When do I have to invite the girl of my bachelor friends? I'm sick of extending welcome after welcome – and I can't tell how important they are.

If they are engaged, if she has cooked a meal for you in his flat or if the man asks to bring her, come she must. Otherwise you can go on treating him as a spare man, though if you think the thing is turning serious it's wise as well as kind to ask her occasionally: 'Be nice to the girls', as Lady Montdore said, 'You never know who

59

they'll marry.' Of course you can go on asking anyone not actually through the vestry for eleventh hour holes in dinner parties – but in those circumstances you can ask grass widowers, boys of 12 or the man who came to mend the electricity, come to that.

Can I bring my girl?

If she's in fact your, er, common-law wife, you can almost insist. If she's just a bird in the by-going, don't unless you know it's a biggish party. But make no mistake about it – a hostess is never pleased. A spare man is always too hard to come by.

I know professional people loathe having their brains picked at parties, but do I really have to ring up a solicitor and make an appointment to deal with a quick question that could be disposed of across the dinner table?

You're dead right, they hate it – there's a classic story of a doctor grousing to a solicitor about this, who asked him what he did when so cornered; and the solicitor said he always sent in a bill later. The doctor thanked him warmly – and got a bill the next day.

The best way out is to ask him if he'll swap one question for a bottle of wine. He can't very well refuse, though he never expects to see the wine – then he's delighted when the well-chosen bottle arrives.

What do you call a woman?

Widows *hate* being suddenly called Mrs Mary Smith instead of Mrs John Smith, if only because divorcees generally are known as Mrs Mary Smith. Some professional women whose names are known get called Mrs Mary Smith, too – but make sure it *is* Mrs Mary Smith and not Mrs Joe Soap. The rudest thing you can ever do to the husband of a professional woman, by the way, is not to address his wife by her professional name – that's understandable. But to do it when you can't remember his too is unforgivable.

How do I get the guests to start moving towards the table once the food is ready?

Have the kitchen ringer go off loudly and leap to your feet. By the time they get downstairs and discover it's cold ham and salad they'll have forgotten what got them on the move anyway.

What does a woman on her own do about eating out? Or even playing host to another woman? We are all right in the YWCA cafeteria, but at more exclusive places we are regularly parked at small tables behind pillars and ignored.

Women are badly treated in restaurants mainly because of the suspicion (not always ill-founded) that they are going to eat the cheapest things, fail to order wine and tip badly. You can't do much to undo this impression for the whole female sex, but you can correct it in your case *if* you stick to the same restaurant for long

I think I've forgotten what a waiter looks like...

enough for them to get the message. This is what female PROs do who are obliged (it says here) to be constantly impressing their clients with high-class nosh. And do watch that tip. Somehow we can work out our 10–15% all right up to about a pound, and then we just can't believe it can be as much as it is. Tip half a crown a pound, and when in doubt make it more not less.

When they say what would you like to drink, they often don't say what. How on earth do you know if it's beer or cocoa?

Play it back at them: say 'What do you suggest?' or 'What are you having?' And if you have asked for the thing they haven't got, try and pretend you really wanted what they are now offering but didn't like to ask – 'Oh I'd *love* coffee, I thought it was too much trouble' or 'BEER! Goodness yes I'm so thirsty.'

*Since you get sneered at one way and another for
every euphemism there is, how should I ask for the
lavatory?*

Every phrase I could think up would become
unsmart if it became at all common; be on your
guard against things like 'the geography', 'the
little girls' room' or (if an absent-minded mother)
asking if you can do a wee-wee. Try 'I'd like to
disappear, if I may' and just hope the gods don't
take you literally.